PINK

By Patricia M. Stockland
Illustrated by Julia Woolf

Content Consultant
Susan Kesselring, MA
Literacy Educator and K-1 Teacher

magic
wagon

(COLORS)

visit us at www.abdopublishing.com

Published by Magic Wagon, a division of the ABDO Publishing Group, 8000 West 78th Street, Edina, Minnesota 55439. Copyright © 2011 by Abdo Consulting Group, Inc. International copyrights reserved in all countries. All rights reserved. No part of this book may be reproduced in any form without written permission from the publisher.

Looking Glass Library™ is a trademark and logo of Magic Wagon.

Printed in the United States of America, North Mankato, Minnesota.
082010
012011

Text by Patricia M. Stockland
Illustrations by Julia Woolf
Edited by Nadia Higgins
Series design by Nicole Brecke
Cover and interior layout by Emily Love

Library of Congress Cataloging-in-Publication Data
Stockland, Patricia M.
  Pink / by Patricia M. Stockland ; illustrated by Julia Woolf.
     p. cm. — (Colors)
  ISBN 978-1-61641-138-1
  1. Pink—Juvenile literature. 2. Colors—Juvenile literature. I. Woolf, Julia. II. Title.
  QC495.5.S7736 2011
  535.6—dc22
                              2010013991

We have an invitation to a tea party.

The invitation is pink.

4

I put on my favorite dress.

My favorite dress is pink.

Mom helps us find our fancy shoes.

Our fancy shoes are pink.

My sister wears a bracelet.

The bracelet is pink.

The table is set for the tea party.

The squares in the tablecloth are pink.

Mom pours tea for my sister and me.

The teacups are pink.

I give my sister a cupcake.

The frosting is pink.

15

My sister gives Teddy
her sparkly scarf.

The sparkly scarf is pink.

We make Mom a crown.

The crown is pink.

Mom gives us each a kiss.

The kisses are pink!

What Is Pink?

There are three primary colors: red, blue, and yellow. These colors combine to create other colors. When you mix red with white, that makes pink.

Primary Colors

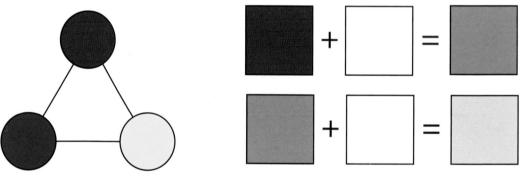

Add a little white, and that makes hot pink. Add a lot of white, and you get light pink. What pink things did you see in this book?

Words to Know

bracelet—jewelry you wear around your wrist.

invitation—a letter asking you to come to a party.

sparkly—giving off a lot of light, the way diamonds do.

tablecloth—a large cloth that covers a table.

Web Sites

To learn more about the color pink, visit ABDO Group online at **www.abdopublishing.com**. Web sites about the colors are featured on our Book Links page. These links are routinely monitored and updated to provide the most current information available.